Teaching Strategies & Techniques for Adjunct Faculty

Fifth Edition

Donald Greive, Ed.D.

Order Information:

Part-Time Press
P.O. Box 130117
Ann Arbor, MI 48113-0117
Part-TimePress.com
PH   734-930-6854
FAX 734-665-9001
ISBN 10-digit 0-940017-12-1
ISBN 13-digit 978-0-940017-12-2

Printed in the United States of America

PREFACE

With the ever increasing numbers of part-time and adjunct faculty teaching today, institutions are assuming more responsibility in providing support and assistance to them. The expertise and experience of part-time faculty are becoming increasingly important to students and institutions. This expertise, however, can only be adequately appreciated if it is recognized and incorporated into the instructional process.

This document has been prepared specifically to assist adjunct faculty, who have careers outside of education, in efficiently grasping concepts necessary for effective teaching.

Realizing the time constraints facing part-time faculty, this book is intentionally brief and to the point. Individuals interested in examining the teaching process in greater detail may find the companion publication, *A Handbook for Adjunct/Part-time Faculty and Teachers of Adults*, of value. It is the hope of the author and publisher that, in some small way, this publication will assist faculty in achieving a successful and rewarding teaching experience.

Donald Greive, Ed.D.

CONTENTS

Instructional Aids ···· 25

Using Technology ···· 28

Planning ···· 31

Testing and Grading ···· 37

Faculty Self-Evaluation ···· 40

Conclusion ···· 43

References ···· 44

List of Figures

INTRODUCTION

This book has been written to efficiently present teaching strategies and techniques. It is purposely brief to provide adjunct/part-time* faculty a quick and straightforward reference. Most of the topics discussed here are covered in greater depth in The Handbook for Adjunct and Part-time Faculty and Teachers of Adults.

As an adjunct faculty member, you make a significant contribution to your institution and to the students who take your classes. Regardless of your reason for teaching, your effectiveness will depend upon the amount of pleasure you experience as a teacher. If you are new or returning to the classroom after being away, you will find that student expectations of college instruction have changed considerably. You'll find this book full of tips, strategies, and proven techniques that address teaching in the contemporary classroom, making your teaching experience productive and enjoyable. So let's get on with it...

* For the purposes of this publication the terms adjunct and part-time faculty are used interchangeably.

Who am I????

... A part-time faculty member!

If I'm early, no one notices ...
... If I'm late, everyone does.
If I'm well-prepared for 101 ...
... I'm assigned 102.
If I have 25 handouts prepared ...
... there are 26 in the class.
If I'm well-prepared...
... the class is cancelled.
If I'm under-prepared ...
... 53 students register.

But I am invaluable! In fact, in some institutions I am responsible for 50 percent or more of the total credit hours taught. I teach anytime, any section, any students. Often, I teach after a full day of work or homemaking. Equally as often, I bring new skills, energy and expertise to the institution where I teach.

Why do I teach? ... I want to share my experience, talents, and skills with others; I want to help bridge the gap between the academic world and the surrounding community; I want to explore new frontiers of learning; ... and I love it.

 Check for the KEY icon when reading this booklet. The KEY is used to highlight special techniques and key concepts to improve your teaching.

FACULTY CHECKLIST

So, you've accepted a position as an adjunct faculty member, received your class assignment, and signed your contract. Listed below are some points you'll want to review with your supervisor prior to beginning your first day of class. Add additional items to create your own personal checklist.

1. Have I completed all my paperwork for employment?
2. Is there a department course syllabus, course outline, or statement of goals and objectives available for the course?
3. How do I get a copy of the text and any ancillary materials for teaching the class?
4. When are grades due and when do students receive grades?
5. Is there a college and/or departmental grading policy?
6. Are there prepared department handouts?
7. Are there prepared department tests?
8. What are the library's book checkout and Internet procedures?
9. What instructional aids are available?
10. What are the bookstore's policies?
11. Is there a college and/or department attendance or tardiness policy?
12. Where can I get instructional aid materials such as films, videotapes, etc., and what is the lead time for ordering?
13. What are the names of the department chairperson, dean, department secretaries, learning resource and support staff, and other significant college officials and how can I reach them, if needed?
14. Have course objectives been reviewed to incorporate the latest technology?
15. Who are some of the other faculty who have taught the course and are they open to assisting adjuncts?

GETTING STARTED

Learning is best accomplished when there is a need to learn and when it builds on prior learning and knowledge. So true learning is as much the responsibility of the student as the teacher. Teachers, however, are an integral part of the learning process and require certain professional skills and competencies. Individuals can no more expect to walk in front of a class without these skills and excel, than one could expect to walk into the middle of an engineering project or legal case and succeed.

The critical difference between teaching and other professions is quite simple. Most professions are very content-oriented, requiring an adequate mastery of subject and a considerable amount of hard work to succeed. In the world of teaching, those factors—while necessary—are useless without possessing the ability to communicate with other human beings.

The basic characteristics of good teaching are:

> Knowing one's subject

> Being able to communicate it effectively

> Knowing and liking students

> Understanding one's culture

Student Characteristics

Today's college teachers encounter few certainties; however, one certainty is that you will face increasingly diverse groups of students. Their backgrounds and aspirations are significantly different from those of the typical "college student" from a few years ago. You must be constantly alert to stereotyping students or classes since it diminishes your chances of success with the group.

Listed on the following page are five common characteristics that may be found in today's college students:

1. The college students of today will probably have a better grasp of where they are going and why they are in class. They may become frustrated if their expectations are not met.
2. Today's college students may view themselves as consumers as well as students. They feel they have purchased a product and they will expect its delivery.
3. They will come to class more mature and more open to sharing their rich life experiences. Many times these experiences can be a valuable asset to the class.
4. They are adults and expect to be treated as such. Very often adult students will rebel at rules and standards that do not seem to contribute to the learning process.
5. Many students have grown up in a culture driven by the fantasy of television, movies, and videos as well as the Internet. This environment may encourage attitudes of disrespect as well as comparisons to professional performers.

In order to challenge these students, instructors need to develop teaching strategies and activities that reach these students, such as group work, cooperative learning, and other activities in which students assume responsibility for themselves and their peers.

Classroom Communication

As pointed out earlier, the principal ingredient of professional teaching is the ability to communicate clearly. In a classroom, communication is more than talking and lecturing. Communication involves eye contact, physical gestures, classroom presence, and proper media and blackboard usage.

Become acquainted with cultural nonverbal communication indicators and, above all, be conscious of any traits that may be construed as offensive or distracting to students. At the same time, you should be conscious of your strengths. Examine and reflect upon your most positive features and mannerisms and incorporate them into your teaching strategies.

& Techniques

And finally, *remember that the three R's of teaching are repeat, respond, and reinforce.* This means that student comments and contributions, if worthy of mention, are worthy of being repeated, responded to and reinforced by the verbal and nonverbal techniques at the command of the teacher.

STRATEGIES FOR TEACHING

Although you may not need to develop a strategic plan for teaching, you should have in your repertoire a variety of approaches to teaching. The following are some contemporary concepts and strategies that have received considerable attention in teaching/learning circles during the past decade.

Andragogy/Pedagogy

With the recent rise in the number of adults attending college, teaching experts have recognized that these new learners brought with them different expectations about their role in the learning process. In fact, it is evident that adults want to play a more active role in their learning experience. In the past, most of us were placed in classes where the teacher determined the activities needed to achieve learning, making the teacher the center of the instructional process. This is called pedagogy and is a vital part of the teaching process. However, experts have realized that pedagogy does not work for all learners in all situations.

Contemporary learners, especially adults, want to be more active in their education. Specifically, they want to know why they must learn something prior to undertaking it; they possess a strong sense of self and feel responsible for their own decisions; and they wish to integrate their life and employment experiences into their learning activities. *These factors influenced the creation of a learner-centered strategy known as andragogy.*

For you as an instructor, the implications are very clear. Your classroom preparation should include learner-centered activities. Many such activities are included here but are not labeled as such. Remember, however, that the andragogical model does not imply that the pedagogical model should be abandoned. There is still a need for pedagogical planning tempered by the concepts of andragogy.

Developing an andragogical teaching strategy requires a classroom that fosters open communication. Be aware that some adults may be anxious about their ability to learn, so plan activities that build student confidence and provide opportunities for students to share their experiences. You must establish yourself as a partner in learning and not an expert who has all of the answers.

 Teaching experts increasingly acknowledge that *students learn from each other as much as from their instructors*. Working together improves all students' achievement in the classroom.

Four important student-centered teaching strategies are cooperative or collaborative learning, partnering, classroom assessment technique, and feedback mechanisms.

Cooperative Learning

Sometimes called collaborative learning, this strategy brings students with differing abilities together in small groups where they reinforce lecture and text material through interaction and discussion. This technique requires detailed planning, including classroom goals, specific activities, and a grading plan. Groups should consist of four or five students. During this activity, the instructor assumes the role of facilitator, maintaining direction and assuring complete student participation.

A good cooperative learning group is established with several conditions. You must make sure all students participate, have a method to capture individual student's participation, and require a tangible result from the group activity.

> The benefits of cooperative learning include:
>
> › students have a vehicle to get to know others in the class (very important for part-time students),
>
> › students develop a commitment to the group,
>
> › grades improve,
>
> › out-of-class group study is encouraged, and
>
> › students become participants in their own learning.

Partnering

In addition to the small group techniques described later, some instructors find that *assigning students to work in pairs or as partners throughout the course greatly enhances their progress.* This technique can be implemented early in the course through voluntary student selection, lottery, or other suitable methods. This system provides each student with a "partner" from whom to seek help and with whom to share ideas as together they proceed through the course.

Student Feedback

One of the most important ways to monitor your success as a teacher is student feedback. Sometimes it is necessary to create formal feedback vehicles rather than to rely upon impressions. In addition to Classroom Assessment Techniques (see below), techniques for obtaining feedback include:

- ☞ Giving sample questions that do not count toward the grade before testing and asking for the correct answer with a show of hands.
- ☞ Making certain there is open and ongoing communication.
- ☞ Asking students to write a letter to the next class describing the course.
- ☞ Having a post-mortem discussion with your class.

Classroom Assessment

Classroom Assessment Techniques (CATs) are based upon a series of teaching techniques in which teachers use classroom research activities to determine what students are learning. They focus on evaluation of instruction and student involvement in the learning process. To be truly developmental, no credit should be granted for CAT activities. Some basic CATs that you can utilize in your classroom are summarized here.

The Minute Paper. At the end of class, ask students to give a written response on the *most important thing they learned and any questions they have concerning the day's topic.* The query can be worded in any manner—remember the response does not count toward the student's grade. If you are seeking a solution to a problem or an analysis of a situation, the question can be worded appropriately. Responses then can be used to start discussion for the next class session.

The Muddiest Point. Students are asked to identify *something about the topic that is confusing.* This question asks the students to identify where you have been unclear. They love this one. You can specify whether the students are to respond to the lecture, a demonstration, or other activity. Remember to specify the activity or you will get general answers of little value.

The One-Sentence Summary. Ask students to *summarize a large amount of information.* This technique is especially effective with important topics and principles. It works well in classes where new concepts are built upon previous lessons. The key question is: "who does what to whom, when, where, how, and why?"

Classroom assessment is closer to doing classroom research than most pedagogical or andragogical techniques. This technique will provide you with a continuous flow of information on student learning and quality of instruction in the classroom. These techniques are discussed in detail in *Classroom Assessment Techniques: A Handbook for College Teachers* (Angelo & Cross, 1992).

Finally, some of the most effective classroom strategies are creative and developed by the instructor. Too often teaching mainly consists of imitating the instructors we had during our own college careers. Such imitation limits the opportunity to try new and different teaching techniques. Many educators feel that *activities in a classroom should change every twenty minutes.* You should not feel obligated to stay with traditional classroom methods. If you feel like taking an innovative approach, share it with your students! They will usually be cooperative and appreciate that you are a risk taker and instructional innovator.

STUDENT CLASSROOM BEHAVIORS

Certainly, teaching is a demanding activity. Most professionals can succeed with knowledge of the technical and intellectual content of their professions. A teacher, however, requires these competencies plus the ability to communicate with large numbers of individuals with divergent learning and behavior patterns. This section discusses some of the more common student behaviors in today's classrooms.

The Class Expert

The class expert has comments and knowledge concerning nearly any topic discussed in class. Be careful not to "put down" these students because it will discourage other students from contributing. Usually, an effective technique is to allow the expert to respond, then let peer pressure in the form of other student responses to eventually limit the expert's comments. If this approach does not solve the problem, an individual conference after the second or third class may be necessary. If all else fails, a verbal request for consideration of the other students during class would be in order. Prepared objectives, to which everyone's attention must be addressed, are a vital asset in curbing the class expert.

The Silent Class

Adjunct instructors commonly encounter silent classes because they are most likely to be teaching older and/or insecure students. Nonetheless, it is important that students be involved vocally in the class. Conversation and involvement are important to the learning process and provide feedback for the teacher. As stated earlier, the *first class can be important in breaking the silence barrier before it starts.* Some techniques to implement communication include: small group work, partnering, discussions of current events and personal experiences, brainstorming, icebreakers, and instructor anecdotes.

The Negative Student

Negative student behavior manifests itself in diverse ways. Sometimes students will challenge class discussion in a negative manner, or in other situations, they merely remain silent and appear to sulk for no apparent reason. It is important that you not allow the negative student syndrome to affect the class. The silent negative student usually will not greatly affect the class; however, the vocal negative student will. Initially, efforts should be made to involve the negative student in a positive or success-oriented question/answer format. Through this technique, you may be able to assess the interests of a negative student and stimulate participation. (Remember, the negative student made the effort to register for the course and to attend the class; thus he or she brings positive attributes.) An individual conference with the student often can clarify and help resolve the matter.

The Unruly Student

Although it is not commonplace, students occasionally surface even in the classroom. Inappropriate behavior can manifest itself in disagreements with other students (possibly physical), verbal outbursts, cursing, or general disruption. You should exhaust all reasonable strategies to control the situation, such as making eye contact with the student, politely asking for cooperation, or private consultation. If conditions reach the point where classroom order can no longer be maintained, ask the rest of the class to leave the room and then address the student with the problem directly in concert with procedures established by the institution.

MOTIVATION

One of the most widely accepted motivational theories is Maslow's hierarchy of needs. This hierarchy also applies to the learning process. It states that basic human needs fall into five categories: physiological, safety, love and belonging, esteem, and self-actualization. Although faculty cannot greatly affect the first three of these needs, they can be effective in developing the final two.

Fostering self-esteem in individuals is accomplished by creating a class environment based upon the "success" concept. Teachers who build the learning experience around student success will find themselves in a productive learning/teaching situation.

Several ideas for developing a success-oriented classroom are:

> Make students aware of your expectations.

> Give students nonverbal encouragement.

> Provide students with positive reinforcement.

> Provide a structured situation in which students will feel comfortable.

> Allow students to discuss their experiences, especially if your classroom contains adult students.

Self-actualization occurs when a student's self-concept is developed. It is most easily realized through achievement and success. You can assist the student in achieving self-actualization in the following ways:

1. Present some kind of challenge in each class, but do not create insurmountable barriers.

2. Treat your students as individuals. Make every effort to prevent your class from becoming impersonal.

3. Do not prejudge or stereotype students. Don't label students or classes as "good" or "bad."

4. Treat your students as adults.

5. Give consideration to students' personal problems. Remember, adult students bring with them all the problems of life outside the classroom as well as those in your class.

6. **Provide a flexible classroom.** Rigid rules are considered demeaning by students. The flexible instructor is a more effective teacher. Being flexible does not imply the loss of authority. The teacher is always the authority in the classroom.

CLASSROOM TECHNIQUES

The First Class

It is normal when you face your first class to experience a certain amount of anxiety. Most teachers feel that this is a positive force that sharpens their skills. Here are some basic guidelines that will assist you in overcoming anxiety and in creating an effective and productive first meeting.

- ∞ Be overprepared rather than underprepared.

- ∞ Plan an activity that gets students involved immediately, such as an information-gathering exercise.

- ∞ Initiate casual conversation with and among students before going into the course specifics.

- ∞ Recount a personal anecdote or bring up a current news or college event to bridge the communication gap.

- ∞ Acknowledge students' confusion at the beginning of class. Confusion is not necessarily detrimental; it can be used to reduce student anxieties.

- ↜ Present the syllabus on an overhead and as a hand-out. Discuss it in detail with the class, emphasizing the sections describing student requirements.

- ↜ Conduct a full class. Teaching a full class creates the impression you're serious about the course.

- ↜ Be prepared with icebreakers, class-related questions with no specific answer, to stimulate discussion.

- ↜ Take care of housekeeping items such as office and restroom locations, if and when there are breaks, etc.

- ↜ Don't hesitate to share your background with the class. This shows you are as willing to share information as to gather it. But don't ask students for more about their backgrounds than you are willing to give about yours.

- ↜ Set the tone of the classroom by creating positive feelings about the course and your expectations for the class.

- ↜ Communicate to the class that you are a friendly, helpful person and not an inflexible disciplinarian.

- ↜ Don't fall into either of these two extremes in classroom behavior: the traditionally rigid "stay in your place" strategy and the laissez-faire "what shall we do today, gang" approach. Seek some happy medium.

The Lecture

The lecture is the most used and the most efficient of teaching techniques. Do not hesitate to use this technique even though it has the reputation of being overused. You must keep in mind that a good lecture can require more preparation than a good group activity or demonstration. Some of the requirements for preparing an effective lecture include:

∞ Carefully preparing notes, examples, formulae and facts, a main theme for the day, and summary. Tell your students where you're going and when you get there.

∞ Making certain that the lecture is directed to the level of the students.

∞ Using anecdotes, concrete examples, and dramatic contrast to emphasize points.

∞ Using gestures and eye contact to keep communication channels open with the class.

∞ Using questions to stimulate and motivate students. Use questions to summarize at the conclusion of every major part of the lecture.

∞ Being conscious of your vocabulary. This is especially important for instructors in specialized areas where professional jargon and buzzwords may not be familiar to students.

∞ Intermixing teaching activities and lecture techniques. Use a combination of traditional lecture, brainstorming, problem solving and discussions. The old one-way lecture gets tiring for both you and your students.

∞ Taking advantage of all the teaching aids available, including audio/visual equipment, instructional technologies, and supplemental materials.

∞ Telling the students at the start what your intentions are and when you are changing topics.

∞ Summarizing—bring the lecture to a close with a summary review of major points or concepts. An effective summary includes repetition and reinforcement of the important points covered.

 It is important to *plan and develop proper lecture techniques.* Unfortunately lectures don't just happen, although many teachers in the past taught that way.

Teaching experts note several characteristics of good lectures:

> Students retain more of the material presented early in lectures, so make important points early and then expand upon them later.

> Lecture presentations are best supported with anecdotes, references, and handouts.

> Important points should be cued before they are presented.

> A lecture no longer means that only the teacher talks. Allow time during the lecture for student feedback, questions, and discussion.

Question/Answer

The intelligent use of questions is probably the most effective teaching mechanism in existence. Proper questioning is the ultimate in good communication because it elicits critical thinking. There are several points to remember in questioning:

෮ Ask an individual a specific question, do not direct general questions to the entire class. After asking the question, pause and wait for the answer.

෮ **Use questions for all purposes**: to arouse curiosity, to assess the students' understanding of your presentation, to evaluate the comprehension of individuals, to allow students to provide input, and to digress from the class contribution.

෮ Use questions creatively whenever possible. A key question or an unusual question in each class session (even making a production of it) effectively stimulates classes and conveys information.

ℛ **Use open-ended questions to supplement lecture.** These questions get students to comment or respond to the opening rather than give short answers. These types of questions would be: "What do you think of that?" or "How does that strike you?" Then call upon individual students by name. Avoid yes/no questions.

Discussion

Good discussion techniques have become a major part of good teaching. Discussions facilitate understanding as well as application and reinforcement. There are several points that should be remembered in developing a discussion plan:

ℛ There must be an objective or purpose for the discussion; otherwise it will deteriorate into a meaningless gab session or an aimless sharing of opinions.

ℛ A case study is an excellent vehicle for developing a meaningful discussion.

ℛ A controversial issue is effective as long as students reach logical conclusions that can be expressed in writing.

ℛ It is a good idea to involve students in the development of the discussion, including: planning the activities, monitoring the discussion, and presenting conclusions.

ℛ Participation in discussion should count toward a student's final grade and should be clearly explained in the evaluation plan of the course so students know exactly the value of their contribution.

Student Panels

A student panel can be used as an alternative to lecturing by giving groups of students the opportunity to do the presenting. However, it must be structured so the specific objectives of the assignment are clearly defined prior to the panel presentation. Normally, a panel should consist of two to four members. Each member of the panel should be assigned specific topics or issues to be presented and/or defended. After the presentation, the rest of the class should be divided into discussion groups so these students can define their positions on the panel's topic. Instructors should remember to help students in developing open-ended questions for the rest of the class. A carefully structured panel is a valuable learning experience for the participants as well as the class.

Learning Cells

In learning cells, students work in pairs to help each other learn; typically, the entire class is paired off for this activity. The pairs can work together in many different ways. It may involve a reading assignment in which the students share what they have read and then develop questions to present to one another. In this case they are demonstrating their reading comprehension and understanding of the issues while sharing their responses. Another possibility uses an open-question format where students can exercise their creativity in their responses or in a problem-solving situation. During the process the teacher moves about the room, going from pair to pair, seeking feedback and answering questions. Learning cells can be organized for an entire term or may be assigned for a single class meeting.

Buzz Groups

As an in-class activity, the buzz group's purpose is to solve a specific problem or compare and contrast an issue. The instructor identifies the discussion topic or problem and allows students to form small groups, usually of three to five students. The students develop their own discussion guidelines for reaching a solution to the issue. The solution is prepared for presentation, possibly on a flip chart or overhead transparency for the following class session. Occasionally the instructor may have a solution prepared and use it as a discussion of the differences between the student buzz groups' and the instructor's conclusions. Buzz groups should not be confused with small group projects.

Buzz groups can be used as a quick conclusion activity that takes only 10 to 15 minutes of class time.

Out-of-Class Activities

Outside Readings/Written Assignments

Outside readings and additional assignments can be used by part-time instructors in several ways. Since neither the instructor nor the student is on campus for extensive library use, outside readings and references should be listed in the syllabus. It will aid part-time students significantly if materials and periodicals selected are available in public libraries or on the Internet. The preparation of handouts with reference numbers will also assist students. This allows students to spend their time in the library actually using the materials rather than searching for them. Again, *being specific in terms of the topic and objectives (and points counted toward the grade) is necessary for a successful outside reading assignment.*

Projects

Student projects are one way students can get the opportunity to learn outside the classroom. Projects may consist of in-depth research into a class topic or a community-based activity such as agency visitations, interviews, or case studies. A properly developed project should allow students to choose from a variety of related activities within their own sphere of interest. After topics are selected, instructor expectations for completion of the project should be clarified. The project should weigh significantly in the final evaluation and assignment of a grade.

Case Studies

Traditionally case studies have been used mainly in sociology or psychology classes. *The case study may, however, be used in many other disciplines.* Students may be given case studies of individuals or processes in finance, investing, historic contrast, geology and other class situations. In a good case study, the instructor establishes the scenario, the objectives of the case, and the problem(s) that may be encountered. Students may then be given time to read and research the project and write their case paper or make an oral presentation which can lead to student discussions that reach consensus or a conclusion. Case studies are normally assigned to individual students and not to groups.

Field Trips

Field trips should be planned so that the entire session of the field trip is on location. The class activities and trip objectives should be outlined prior to the trip. Arrange the class in small groups and specify to the students what they are to observe. At the conclusion of the visit, meet to discuss the major points observed and any conclusions to be made. The most effective field trips include credit toward the grade and require a written or oral report.

INSTRUCTIONAL AIDS

Recent studies demonstrate that student retention of information improves markedly when faculty make use of appropriate instructional aids. Modern technology has opened a new vista of tools for use in the classroom. However, there are still some tried and true instructional aids available to you. A few examples are listed below. Some of the guidelines governing the use of such aids include making certain that *instructional aids support the lesson objective, build on previous learning, appeal to students and maintain student attention, contain quality graphs, text and photos as required and encourage student participation when appropriate.*

Projected Material

Traditional aids in this group include movies & short films, slides of various sizes, transparencies for overhead projection, and specialized equipment such as computer projection or an opaque projector. However, the use of movies, short films and filmstrips for training has declined, mostly because of availability of more user-friendly media such as video. The essential factor governing continued use is that the content must be current and support the lesson. Aside from a chalk or marker board, the overhead transparency and projector is still one of the more convenient and cost effective instructional aids.

The overhead projector has become one of the most popular support tools in education because it allows instructors to face the class while showing images on a screen using normal room lighting. Overhead projectors are inexpensive and are usually readily available from the academic division office or the audio/visual department. Some projectors are equipped with a roll that provides a continuous writing surface. This enables the retention of information on the roll in the event students later wish to discuss specific points, and is especially useful in mathematics, engineering, etc., classes.

There is no limit to the artistic excellence that can be produced on a transparency. Many faculty members easily prepare their own transparencies. Transparencies may be typewritten, handwritten, computer-generated, or drawn on standard-size plain white paper and instantaneously produced on a standard copier. Many times it is worth the extra effort to make a professional-looking overhead transparency. They are easily maintained, durable, and thus can become a permanent part of future presentations.

Video

For instructors, the convenience of DVD video is certainly an advantage. The capability to easily stop, freeze, zoom, and replay is particularly helpful for both instructors and students.

Probably the most effective modern instructional aid is the DVD (or videotape). With the reduction in cost of digital camcorders and digital production, the possibilities for expanded use are nearly endless. Most institutions now have equipment for instructors who wish to develop their own video clips as well as a library of DVDs and tapes that may be applicable to your class. Videos are not only attention getters, but provide the opportunity for direct student involvement when students produce their own videos. However, *instructors must indicate to the students the objectives behind any videos and combine the video with discussion, a written report, or other activity.*

Interactive Video

Interactive video refers broadly to software that responds quickly to certain choices and commands by the user. A typical system consists of a combination of a compact disk, computer, and video technology. Well-designed interactive video, when properly used, is highly effective as an instructional aid. Each student essentially receives a customized learning experience.

Computer-Based Multimedia

Interactive video is one form of computer-based multimedia. However, the terms computer-based training (CBT), or multimedia training, have become very popular. The term multimedia is not new. Multimedia has been used for decades in some form or other. In a basic form, multimedia is a combination of more than one instructional media, but it could include several forms of media-audio, text, graphics, and video (or film). Although computers are often used on an individual basis by students, equipment is available that can project images from a computer screen. This allows the instructor to use a computer in conjunction with specially designed software programs to create presentations for an entire class. The instructor can tailor the presentation for the class, if necessary, and also include graphics at appropriate points.

Flipcharts

A common visual aid used in business seminars is the simple flipchart. When adapted to the classroom, the flipchart has many advantages over a chalkboard or overhead projector. The flipchart, a large tablet with pages that can be flipped vertically, is especially useful for small groups to record their discussions and conclusions. Instructors can record major points of a presentation and have room to add notes, descriptions, or comments. The information can then be retained by tearing off the page and taping it to the wall for future reference. A flipchart and felt-tip pen can be one of the most effective tools in the active classroom.

Handouts

Print media, including photographs, reproductions of pictures, drawings, murals, cartoons, and other print materials are valuable supplemental aids. Charts, diagrams, and graphs are also in this category. Many of these items are suitable for long-term use. Although sometimes overused in the past, handouts are still a valuable instrument for instructors. PDF and other document production software make preparing and updating easy. Handouts should be used for material that students will need for reference, such as important definitions, computations, or position statements for discussion. Handouts for lecture purposes should only contain an outline of the material discussed with space for students to add their own comments.

A serious note of caution: be careful of copyright violations! Your supervisor or department head should be able to provide you with the Fair Use guidelines you will need to follow.

NOTE: When planning to use an instructional aid, be sure you have all the equipment you require before the class begins, whether it's chalk, markers, flipchart easels, masking tape, or the TV/VCR/DVD player to show your tape.

USING TECHNOLOGY

The technological revolution has not bypassed the college classroom. Whether you have the need or opportunity to utilize technology, your students' have grown up with it, and their mastery of it will impact your teaching. All of your students will have surfed the Net, used chat rooms, Instant Messaging (IM), social networking sites (Facebook, Twitter, etc...) and e-mail.

There are three specific areas where computers can be used to improve the learning process. All instructors should be familiar with them. They are presentation software, the Internet, and e-mail.

Presentation Software

Presentation software, as the name suggests, presents classroom material in a format similar to an overhead projector, saves the presentation, and allows changes that reflect student participation or new information. One of the most popular types of presentation software is PowerPoint™ published by Microsoft. PowerPoint™ is here to stay. At 20-years-old, it is still the leading presentation software. At one point it was estimated that there are 30 million PowerPoint™ presentations given every day. However, there are other products available, as well. These include Apple Keynote™ for Mac users, and Adobe Photoshop™. Open Office Impress™ is a free open source presentation technology. It contains a number of features not available in PowerPoint™.

Presentation software as a teaching aid improves instruction by:

> building a knowledge base for class discussion or as reinforcement of your presentation,

> increasing the comprehension level of key concepts,

> analyzing complex material through data utilization, and assessing instructional quality through summary.

Internet

Finding information on the Internet is second nature to all students. Making good use of the Internet requires fundamental research skills as well as the ability to use Internet search engines such 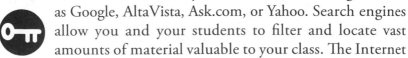 as Google, AltaVista, Ask.com, or Yahoo. Search engines allow you and your students to filter and locate vast amounts of material valuable to your class. The Internet comes with several cautions, however. *If you require term papers, you must set up safeguards that keep your students from obtaining the entire paper off the Internet. One way to avoid this is to require analysis and synthesis in the paper.* Another danger is that anything can be put on the Internet; some of it factual, some invalid and inaccurate. Control this by recommending reliable websites and sources acceptable for student use.

Course Websites

About half of all faculty create course websites that provide more detailed information about what their courses cover. These websites generally include details about course requirements, texts, and other resources and can be a valuable resource for students. Course websites can include audio and video materials, as well as downloadable files. Keep in mind, however, that a course website should be kept up to date, but once designed and launched course websites can be invaluable tools. Your college may provide templates. This site (http://www.indiana.edu/~tltl/instrweb/templts.html) at Indiana University offers a trio of instructional website templates.

E-mail

Every college or university has e-mail capability and most encourage adjunct faculty to use their systems. Whether or not your institution encourages e-mail communication, establish an e-mail address as soon as possible. A word of caution, however. Make certain that all students have access to e-mail and manage your teaching e-mail by establishing a unique address available to all students (separate from the address to which your non-teaching e-mail goes).

A simple e-mail application to help communicate with students is establishing a listserv for your class. *A listserv allows you and anyone in your class to communicate with the entire class simultaneously by posting a single message.* The ultimate in communication, of course, is the creation of electronic discussion groups for your students.

PLANNING

In teaching, experts and practitioners universally agree that one element ranks highest in importance: planning. Adequate planning is essential to reaching the desired learning outcomes. Teachers who depend upon "off-the-cuff" teaching are doomed to fail. Although there are many planning support mechanisms, all are essentially built upon one premise—to adequately outline the class step-by-step. Prior to embarking upon the planning process, however, it is important to develop specific objectives for the course. *Properly stated*

 objectives not only provide guidelines for both the teacher and the student throughout the course, they prevent students from deviating from course content.

There are structured methods for the development of a proper course plan. The simplest method begins with the catalog description of the course you are teaching. This should help you decide upon the broad goals for the course. Then under each goal you can list your objectives. Properly written objectives will use such descriptors as write, solve, contrast, compare, describe, identify, and list. Do not use general descriptors such as enjoy, appreciate, discuss, believe, and grasp because there is no way to evaluate them.

Most courses can be adequately covered in eight to twelve objectives. Writing too many objectives leads to a lack of clear direction in the course.

There are three major components to creating a formal teaching plan: the course outline, the lesson plan, and the course syllabus.

> The lesson plan is the instrument the instructor uses day-to-day, the course outline is the instructor's guideline to course content, and the syllabus is to some degree a combination of the two.

Course Outline

Whereas the lesson plan is a daily map for teachers to ensure their direction in a given session, the course outline is much more comprehensive and allows you to monitor the flow of the entire course. The outline normally is created from the course objectives. An outline format is usually used with no greater detail than a list of objectives with two or three subtopics under each.

When developing an outline, you must determine whether the course needs to be structured in a chronological or topical format. *A chronological format requires that fundamentals be mastered before moving on to more advanced concepts, whereas a topical outline can be modified and rearranged with much more flexibility* because there is no concern that students have prior knowledge.

Lesson Plan

The format for the lesson varies depending upon the instructor and the type of course being taught. The only thing universally agreed upon is that the lesson plan should be written down. Each plan should list a definite purpose that gives the main points of the lesson, and each should be numbered and arranged as part of the total plan for the course. For example, references, research, and quotes may be part of the formal lesson plan, while anecdotal comments may be written in as marginal notes, and outside references such as newspaper clippings handled as unique entities.

Ask yourself the question that students often ask—What are we going to do today—and why?

A lesson plan is made up of a number of parts
They are:

> A list of definitions for explanation
> The objectives of the class
> The impact or purpose of the class
> A definite plan for instructor activities
> The outline of student activities
> The assignment for the next session

Below is a lesson plan model you can use in preparing for classes.

LESSON PLAN

Course number and name _____

Date_____

Session # _____

Topic(s) to be covered _____

_____

Instructional aids, materials_____

Definitions to be covered _____

_____

Class objective(s) _____

_____

Student activities or exercises _____

_____

Instructor activities _____

_____

Major impact or thought _____

Assignment _____

_____

The lesson plans for a course should be accumulated and kept chronologically in a permanent file or notebook to eliminate the need to develop a completely new lesson plan each time you teach the same course. Maintained in chronological order, they are available for easy reference and for review and update as each new class begins. Reviewing your lesson plans eliminates dated and irrelevant material.

Syllabus

A syllabus is defined as "a concise statement of the main points of a course of study or subject" and is considered the official document for the course. It should be shared with students and should be a permanent part of the college's instructional archives. It may even become a legal document in case of litigation.

Despite universal recognition of the syllabus' importance in course preparation and instruction, no single format has wide acceptance. While there is wide variation in the content of the syllabus, most faculty agree that a syllabus should contain these main parts:

1. The **complete name of the course**, including the course number and section.

2. **Course description**. A narrative description of the course based upon the college catalog description.

3. The **faculty member's name** and preferred title.

4. The **faculty member's availability**. This should include: office hours, meeting location, phone, and e-mail address. Include procedures for arranging an appointment since most adjunct faculty do not have individual offices.

5. The **required materials**. This should include the text(s), outside readings and manuals, reference materials, supplies, and web page addresses, if applicable.

6. Any **course requirements and prerequisites**.

7. The **course objectives**. Be specific. Clarify and articulate the objectives that the students will achieve by the end of the course. Number them for emphasis.

8. The **specific assignments**, projects, etc., to be completed by the students.

9. A **complete listing of outside resources**, readings, and group activities, etc.

10. **Attendance policy**. Clarify expectations concerning tardiness and quiz/test makeups.

11. **Classroom regulations**. This should include academic honesty, behavior expectations, harassment and general operational procedures.

12. **Evaluation plan and grading standards**. Specify the weighting of all graded assignments: tests, quizzes, class participation, projects, group work evaluation, and field trips, etc.

13. **Emergency procedures**. Include emergency phones, evacuation procedures, medical assistance, and campus security.

The syllabus should be distributed to the students on the first day of class. Time should be taken to discuss the details of the syllabus. In fact, it is good practice to go over the syllabus during the second meeting of the class. *Describe in detail the student activities and how they relate to certain assignments and objectives. Remember that a syllabus is an essential part of any course and it should be shown that respect in its development and use.*

First Time Teacher Revelation #27

"The mediocre teacher tells. The good teacher explains. The superior teacher demonstrates. The great teacher inspires."
—William Arthur Ward

Evaluation Plan & Charting

An evaluation plan that is understood by all students is necessary for the proper assignment of grades. The evaluation plan is a simple chart that contains all of the factors used in the assignment of grades. The simplest and most easily understood plan is one that assigns points for each element graded. This is easy to understand and requires only simple arithmetic to arrive at an accurate grade assignment. A sample chart is shown below:

EVALUATION CHART			
Grade Factors	Percent of Final Grade	Possible Points	Points Received
Test #1	15	30	26
Test #2	15	30	28
Test #3	30	60	54
Outside Project	10	20	15
Class Participation	10	20	16
Group work	10	20	20
Paper	10	20	20
Total	**100**	**200**	**179**

Note that the grade factors are listed in the first column. In the second column, the percent to be assigned to the final grade is shown. It should always add up to 100. The third column indicates the total number of points possible for each activity. These values are determined by multiplying the total number of points for the course (200) times the assigned percentage. This provides the "weighting" for the different grade factors. Here the total need not add up to 100 but each must reflect the percentages of column 2. Note in the sample evaluation the student earned 179 points of a possible 200. The percentage grade then can easily be obtained by dividing 179 (points earned) by 200 (points possible) or 89.5 percent. Obviously, this simple chart can easily be placed on a computer program for rapid and accurate calculation.

TESTING AND GRADING

The assignment of grades is one of the most important and difficult tasks in teaching. Regardless of the process adopted, it is difficult to eliminate all subjectivity from assigning grades. Thus it is important that the instructor develop the best evaluation and grading skills possible. Modern technology has improved the process, at least for multiple-choice questions, by providing test validity through item analysis techniques.

 Establishing the criteria for grades and sharing it with students as part of the course syllabus starts the evaluation process very early in the course. Described below are the major types of tests and questions used in a complete evaluation plan.

The major types of tests used in college classes are: essay, multiple choice, and recall. In special circumstances, performance, oral, and short-answer tests may also be utilized.

Essay Tests/Questions

Essay tests work at any level of the learning hierarchy by incorporating analysis and synthesis. Although essay tests require considerable time for students, they give significant insight into what the students are learning and what they are hearing in the classroom.

There are several factors to remember when writing test questions that require essay answers:

- ✆ Questions should be related to the written course objectives.

- ✆ Questions should incorporate a significant amount of content.

- ✆ Questions should be worded so excessive time is not spent on trivial matters.

- ✆ The student must have sufficient background to respond adequately to the question.

37

         ∞ Questions should not be ambiguous or deceptive.

         ∞ Questions should not ask for student opinions.

Essay questions, if constructed and graded properly, are the most accurate of the possible testing techniques. Grading essay questions also presents the greatest challenge and *the best way to judge an essay response is for you to write your response, listing important comments by priority. Assigning points to these prioritized criteria will give a degree of grading objectivity.*

Multiple-choice Tests/Questions

Large classes and computerized scoring make multiple-choice tests the most used tests today. In fact, computer programs exist which allow the instructor to change multiple-choice tests for different classes of the same course. This is accomplished by developing a large database of questions and randomly selecting from the database.

The actual construction of the multiple-choice tests has several general guidelines. They include:

    ∞ Do not include answers that are obviously correct or incorrect, including impossible responses or distracters.

    ∞ Be sure the correct answers are scattered throughout the response mechanism.

    ∞ Provide four possible responses to minimize the guess factor.

    ∞ Do not use "all of the above" or "none of the above."

    ∞ Do not use the terms never, always or likely since they may divert the student.

    ∞ Do not include "trick" or misleading questions or overly difficult vocabulary.

    ∞ Present multiple-choice questions positively rather than negatively.

& Techniques

- ✑ Be consistent with the format to avoid confusion.

- ✑ Keep choices approximately the same length since incorrect answers are frequently shorter than correct ones.

Multiple-choice tests measure discrimination abilities as well as simple knowledge and should always deal with a significant aspect of the course.

Recall and Completion Tests/Questions

The compromise between the multiple-choice test and the essay test is the short answer or recall test. Short-answer questions can be written to a specific topic or point and do not require as much time and effort as essay questions, while allowing for the creativity and analysis not permissible with multiple-choice questions.
Some suggestions for developing recall questions are:

- ✑ Give information concerning the answer prior to the answer blank.

- ✑ Qualify information so students are clear about the response.

- ✑ Include responses at the analysis and synthesis level.

- ✑ Pose questions with only one correct response.

- ✑ Allow sufficient space for the response.

- ✑ Avoid patterns of responses.

- ✑ Avoid direct quotes.

- ✑ Avoid specific descriptors or adjectives.

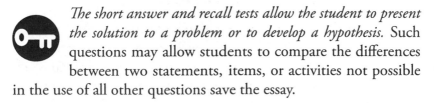 *The short answer and recall tests allow the student to present the solution to a problem or to develop a hypothesis.* Such questions may allow students to compare the differences between two statements, items, or activities not possible in the use of all other questions save the essay.

True/False Tests/Questions

True/false questions are not commonly used at the college level any longer. Although they may have their place in sampling student responses to a learning activity, they generally are not accepted as objective or valid in testing situations.

Regardless of the types of tests used, there are several criteria that must be kept in mind in assigning grades.

> **Communicate the criteria for grades** at the beginning of the course and clarify any misunderstandings then.

> **Include criteria other than test scores** such as class participation, projects, and research.

> **Avoid irrelevant factors** such as tardiness and unexcused absences.

> **Weigh grading criteria carefully**—do not give equal credit for activities that are obviously not equal.

> **Grade students by their individual achievement**, not other students—the "bell curve" standard was abandoned years ago.

FACULTY SELF-EVALUATION

Any dynamic process like teaching is of little value unless it can be assessed to determine if it is achieving its goals. After instructors feel they have adequately planned, expending hours of time and energy, they will want some indication of the fruits of that planning. One method that can be used to evaluate your teaching technique and course structure is with a faculty self-evaluation.

Although most colleges have official faculty evaluation forms that they either require or recommend using, faculty may wish to develop a self-evaluation form.

A few underlying principles for self-evaluations include:

- ↝ The form should not be so long that students eventually check anything to complete the form.

- ↝ It should be logically organized into classroom, course, and instructor evaluation.

- ↝ The evaluation code should be simple and easily understood. Avoid excessive numbering such as 1-10. Students easily understand a simple grading system using A through F.

- ↝ It should, of course, be anonymous and should be given prior to the class session during which the final examination is held.

- ↝ The students should be informed that only constructive criticism and/or reinforcement is of value.

A suggested faculty self-evaluation form is shown below. These are only some of the questions that can be asked and their statistical validity has not been tested. However, it provides suggested guidelines for the development of an instrument for your use.

Even though students are often biased, the value of student input is unquestionable. Most students will respond honestly and sincerely and, over the course of several classes, the statistically deviant responses can be identified and disregarded.

FACULTY EVALUATION FORM

CLASS:_____

DATE: _____

INSTRUCTIONS: Please grade each factor on a scale of A-F in terms of your perception of the teacher's behavior or characteristics.

CLASSROOM EVALUATION

Preparation for class   _____

Communication of classroom expectation   _____

Command of subject matter   _____

Professionalism of classroom behavior   _____

Match of tests and evaluations to course objectives   _____

Encouragement of student participation   _____

Clarity and conciseness of assignments   _____

COURSE-RELATED FACTORS

Course objectives clearly defined   _____

Course content clearly reflects catalog description   _____

Appropriateness of project assignments   _____

Value of field trips   _____

Appropriateness of topic selection for outside assignments   _____

Utilization of supplemental teaching aids, support materials and other props   _____

INSTRUCTOR EVALUATION

Consideration for differing opinions   _____

Consideration for individuals as persons   _____

Willingness to give individual help   _____

Utilized technology and instructional aids   _____

Personal appearance   _____

Instructor's greatest strengths: _____

Instructor's greatest weaknesses: _____

Suggestions to improve course: _____

CONCLUSION

Teaching part-time at the college level can be one of the most rewarding activities you can find. You increase your own knowledge of the course material by reviewing for presentation to students and you gain new skills in communicating that could very well improve your skills at work as well.

THE NON-TRADITIONAL STUDENT

However, you need to take your task as teacher as seriously as you take the other important parts of your life. You are as much responsible for your students learning the material as they are and—you are the one with the control to direct that learning.

By planning, planning, and overplanning, you can feel confident in your abilities to cover the course objectives and to grade your students fairly and without bias. And, if you're unsure about any of your planning instruments, remember that there are others around you who want you to succeed as much as you do. Show your plans to your supervisor, coordinator, or a teacher who you respect.

Getting to know your students and the experiences they bring to your class will give you considerable appreciation for the diversity of your community. Using active learning techniques will bring out these experiences and give all your students the confidence they will need to compete in today's job market.

Now, go teach! And don't forget to have enough confidence to have fun!

REFERENCES

Angelo, T. A., & Cross, P. K. (1992). Classroom Assessment Techniques: A Handbook for College Teachers. San Francisco: Jossey-Bass.

Davis, B. G. (1993). Tools for Teaching. San Francisco: Jossey-Bass.

Greive, D. (2007). A Handbook for Adjunct/Part-time Faculty and Teachers of Adults. Ann Arbor, MI: Part-Time Press.

Knowles, M. (1998). The Adult Learner: A Neglected Species. Houston: Gulf.

McKeachie, W. J. (2001). Teaching Tips, 11th Ed. Boston, MA: Houghton Mifflin.

Sego, A. (1998). Cooperative Learning: Professional's Guide. Westminster, CA: Teacher Created Materials.

ABOUT THE AUTHOR

Donald Greive spent the majority of his educational career as a faculty member and an administrator of part-time faculty. Before retiring, he served as a dean and director of evening and continuing education as well as dean of academic and instructional services. He served as an adjunct faculty member at a liberal arts college, state university, community college, and technical institute. He also managed several national conferences on the topic of adjunct and part-time faculty.

Previously, he edited *Teaching In College: A Resource for Adjunct Faculty.* He recently authored a new edition of *A Handbook for Adjunct/Part-time Faculty and Teachers of Adults.* He founded the journal, *Adjunct Info: A Journal for Managers of Adjunct and Part-time Faculty,* and has served as editor for 10 years.

NOTES

Part-Time Press Instructional Products

Handbook for Adjunct/Part-Time Faculty, 6th Edition *by Donald Greive*
(paperback)

> 1-9 copies $16.00 each
> 10-49 copies $13.00 each
> 50-99 copies $11.00 each
> 100+ copies $9.00 each

Handbook II: Advanced Teaching Strategies *by Donald Greive, Editor*
(paperback)

> 1-9 copies $17.00 each
> 10-49 copies $14.00 each
> 50-99 copies $12.00 each
> 100+ copies $10.00 each

Managing Adjunct/Part-Time Faculty *by Donald Greive & Catherine Worden, ed.*(pb)

> 1-4 copies $25.00 each
> 5-19 copies $20.00 each
> 20+ copies $15.00 each
> (hardcover) *$35.00*

Order online at www.Part-TimePress.com
Order by phone: 734-930-6854

Teaching Strategies and Techniques, Revised 5th Edition
by Donald Greive,

1-9 copies $10.00 each
10-49 copies $8.00 each
50-99 copies $6.25 each
100+ copies $5.00 each

Going the Distance: A Handbook for Part-Time & Adjunct Faculty Who Teach Online, Rev. 1st Ed.
by Evelyn Beck (paperback)

1-9 copies $13.00 each
10-24 copies $10.00 each
25-99 copies $8.75 each
100+ copies $7.50 each

Adjunct Advocate: The e-Zine for Adjunct College Faculty

Single subscription $20.00/year
Library Subscription $199.00/yr

Teaching and Learning in College: A Resource for Educators,
by Gary Wheeler, ed. **$20.00**

Part-Time Press Order Form

Qty	Title	Price
	Subtotal	
	Shipping	
	Total	

Purchaser/Payment Information

☐ Check (payable to Part-Time Press)

☐ Credit Card # _____

 Exp. Date _____

☐ Purchase Order # _____

Name _____

Title _____

Institution _____

Address _____

City/ST/Zip _____

Phone: _____ FAX: _____

E-mail: _____

Shipping and Handling Fee Schedule:

$0-$30 purchase	$ 5.00
$31-$75 purchase	$10.00
$76-$149 purchase	$15.00
Purchases over $150	8% of purchase subtotal

Order online at www.Part-TimePress.com
Order by phone: 734-930-6854